REWARDS *Writing*

Word Choice
Help Book

Anita L. Archer, Ph.D.
Mary M. Gleason, Ph.D.
Stephen L. Isaacson, Ph.D.

Sopris West™
EDUCATIONAL SERVICES

A Cambium Learning Company

BOSTON, MA · LONGMONT, CO

Sopris West™
EDUCATIONAL SERVICES

A Cambium Learning Company

17855 Dallas Parkway, Suite 400 ■ Dallas, TX 75287

(800) 547-6747 ■ www.voyagersopris.com

Contents

BAD *(bad, worse, worst)*

Meaning #1	**bad** can mean *awful*
	James turned in a *bad* paper.
	James turned in an *unacceptable* paper.

Meaning #2	**bad** can mean *harmful*
	The *bad* chemicals might hurt your skin.
	The *dangerous* chemicals might hurt your skin.

Meaning #3	**bad** can mean *evil*
	The *bad* man went to jail.
	The *corrupt* man went to jail.

A.
awful

terrible
atrocious
appalling
worthless
imperfect
unacceptable
unsatisfactory
inadequate
inferior
deficient

B.
harmful

hurtful
injurious
unhealthy
damaging
dangerous
devastating
ruinous
detrimental
destructive
disastrous

C.
evil

mean
wicked
sinful
immoral
unethical
criminal
guilty
corrupt
delinquent
wrong

antonyms: good, strong, harmless

BIG *(big, bigger, biggest)*

Meaning #1	**big** can mean *large*
	The *big* ship entered the bay.
	The *colossal* ship entered the bay.

Meaning #2	**big** can mean *important*
	Paul presented his *big* ideas to the class.
	Paul presented his *valuable* ideas to the class.

A.

large

huge
enormous
gigantic
giant
jumbo
colossal
gargantuan
mammoth
immense
massive
vast
spacious
humongous

B.

important

great
major
main
valuable
significant
tremendous
momentous
outstanding
extraordinary
influential
serious
considerable
prominent

antonyms: little, small, insignificant, unimportant

BORING *(boring, more boring, most boring)*

Meaning #1	**boring** means *uninteresting*
	The *boring* play continued for three hours.
	The *dull* play continued for three hours.

A.

uninteresting

drab
dull
unexciting
tiring
repetitious
tedious
ordinary
unvaried
plain

B.

uninteresting

bland
humdrum
colorless
commonplace
ineffective
unappealing
sluggish
lifeless
insipid

antonym: interesting

BRAVE *(brave, braver, bravest)*

Meaning #1	**brave** means *courageous*
	The *brave* firefighter climbed into the burning house. The *heroic* firefighter climbed into the burning house.

A.

courageous

bold
fearless
gutsy
plucky
daring
reckless
audacious

B.

courageous

unafraid
adventurous
heroic
valiant
gallant
lionhearted
confident

antonyms: afraid, timid, cowardly

BUSY *(busy, busier, busiest)*

Meaning #1	**busy** can mean *hard-working*
	The *busy* shopkeeper worked seven days a week.
	The *industrious* shopkeeper worked seven days a week.

Meaning #2	**busy** can mean *active*
	The *busy* students completed their projects.
	The *energetic* students completed their projects.

A.
hard-working

working
productive
untiring
industrious
enterprising
persevering
occupied
swamped

antonyms: inactive, lazy, idle

B.
active

lively
hectic
bustling
engaged
enthusiastic
energetic
intense
strenuous

CALM (*calm, calmer, calmest*)

Meaning #1	**calm** can mean *peaceful*
	The ship bobbed gently on the *calm* sea.
	The ship bobbed gently on the *unruffled* sea.

Meaning #2	**calm** can mean *patient*
	The *calm* mother ended the sibling fight with ease.
	The *relaxed* mother ended the sibling fight with ease.

A.	**B.**	**C.**
peaceful	**peaceful**	**patient**
quiet	smooth	cool-headed
tranquil	steady	poised
placid	motionless	relaxed
still	unruffled	unemotional
even	undisturbed	level-headed
unmoving	harmonious	unexcitable

antonyms: excited, angry, nervous

CAREFUL *(careful, more careful, most careful)*

Meaning #1	**careful** means *cautious*
	The *careful* baker decorated the cake with delicate flowers.
	The *meticulous* baker decorated the cake with delicate flowers.

A.

cautious

safe
conservative
watchful
observant
attentive
mindful
vigilant

B.

cautious

detailed
painstaking
thorough
diligent
conscientious
accurate
precise

C.

cautious

particular
deliberate
thoughtful
considerate
fussy
meticulous
fastidious

antonyms: reckless, inattentive

CLEAN *(clean, cleaner, cleanest)*

Meaning #1	**clean** can mean *spotless*
	After hours of labor, the kitchen was *clean*.
	After hours of labor, the kitchen was *immaculate*.

Meaning #2	**clean** can mean *tidy*
	When everything was put away, the office was *clean*.
	When everything was put away, the office was *in order*.

Meaning #3	**clean** can mean *sterilized*
	Clean equipment must be used for surgery.
	Disinfected equipment must be used for surgery.

A.	**B.**	**C.**
spotless	**tidy**	**sterilized**
unsoiled	orderly	pure
washed	organized	antiseptic
spick-and-span	arranged	disinfected
immaculate	neat	sterile
sparkling	shipshape	purified
gleaming	uncluttered	unpolluted
unstained	in order	uncontaminated
unsmudged	well-kept	hygienic

antonym: dirty

COLD *(cold, colder, coldest)*

Meaning #1	**cold** can mean *chilly*
	On the *cold* day, snow covered the hills. On the *frigid* day, snow covered the hills.

Meaning #2	**cold** can mean *unfriendly*
	The *cold* girl walked right past the new students. The *indifferent* girl walked right past the new students.

A.

chilly

cool
icy
freezing
bitter
biting
crisp
shivery

B.

chilly

frosty
wintry
nippy
numbing
ice-cold
frigid
frozen

C.

unfriendly

unconcerned
indifferent
joyless
emotionless
reserved
unenthusiastic
unmoved

antonyms: hot, warm

DIRTY *(dirty, dirtier, dirtiest)*

Meaning #1	dirty means *unclean*
	The *dirty* pond no longer supported fish life.
	The *contaminated* pond no longer supported fish life.

A.

unclean

grimy
messy
filthy
stained
muddy
dingy
grubby
grungy

B.

unclean

smudged
smudgy
polluted
contaminated
untidy
soiled
spotted
sloppy

C.

unclean

slimy
nasty
foul
greasy
dusty
mucky
disheveled
murky

antonym: clean

EASY *(easy, easier, easiest)*

Meaning #1	**easy** can mean *not difficult*
	Since the directions were *easy*, the project was completed quickly. Since the directions were *straightforward*, the project was completed quickly.

Meaning #2	**easy** can mean *relaxed*
	There was nothing to do on the *easy* afternoon. There was nothing to do on the *peaceful* afternoon.

A.	**B.**	**C.**
not difficult	**not difficult**	**relaxed**
simple	not troublesome	calm
basic	manageable	peaceful
clear	no bother	unhurried
easily done	painless	comfortable
undemanding	uncomplicated	leisurely
effortless	straightforward	restful

antonyms: hard, difficult, uneasy

EXCITED *(excited, more excited, most excited)*

Meaning #1	excited means *thrilled*
	The *excited* audience clapped as the band took the stage. The *enthusiastic* audience clapped as the band took the stage.

A.

thrilled

enthusiastic
moved
hyper
wild
eager
stimulated
animated

antonym: bored

B.

thrilled

worked up
fired up
stirred up
steamed up
beside oneself
hysterical
frantic

C.

thrilled

aroused
inspired
passionate
nervous
agitated
tumultuous
provoked

FAT *(fat, fatter, fattest)*

Meaning #1	**fat** means *not skinny*
	The *fat* cat sprawled on the couch.
	The *rotund* cat sprawled on the couch.

A.

not skinny

heavy
large
plump
chubby
tubby
beefy
brawny
stout
portly

B.

not skinny

husky
hefty
chunky
overweight
gargantuan
rotund
obese
heavyset
corpulent

antonyms: slender, skinny, thin

FRIENDLY *(friendly, friendli**er**, friendli**est**)*

Meaning #1	friendly means *kind*
	The *friendly* neighbors extended a welcome to the newcomers.
	The *warmhearted* neighbors extended a welcome to the newcomers.

A.

kind

caring
considerate
helpful
loving
warm
warmhearted
kindhearted

B.

kind

pleasant
likeable
favorable
agreeable
neighborly
chummy
affectionate

C.

kind

attentive
loyal
sympathetic
congenial
amiable
intimate
confiding

antonyms: mean, belligerent

(FUNNY) *(funny, funnier, funniest)*

Meaning #1	**funny** can mean *humorous*
	We laughed at the *funny* circus act.
	We laughed at the *hilarious* circus act.

Meaning #2	**funny** can mean *unusual*
	Seeing a house move down the street was *funny*.
	Seeing a house move down the street was *bizarre*.

A.	**B.**	**C.**
humorous	**humorous**	**unusual**
laughable	hysterical	strange
jolly	entertaining	odd
comical	clever	peculiar
comic	absurd	bizarre
amusing	ridiculous	mysterious
witty	ludicrous	curious
hilarious	preposterous	suspicious

antonym: serious

GOOD *(good, better, best)*

Meaning #1	**good** can mean *excellent*
	The handmade tablecloth is *good*.
	The handmade tablecloth is *marvelous*.

Meaning #2	**good** can mean *well-behaved*
	Thirty *good* children waited for the movie to begin.
	Thirty *praiseworthy* children waited for the movie to begin.

Meaning #3	**good** can mean *skilled*
	The electrician was *good*.
	The electrician was *proficient*.

Meaning #4	**good** can mean *useful*
	An electric teapot is *good*.
	An electric teapot is *convenient*.

A. excellent	B. well-behaved	C. skilled	D. useful
fine	obedient	able	helpful
splendid	dutiful	capable	beneficial
superb	honest	talented	acceptable
terrific	honorable	skillful	convenient
wonderful	pure	expert	desirable
marvelous	guiltless	first-rate	favorable
tremendous	innocent	proficient	appropriate
fabulous	respectable	adept	advantageous
desirable	polite	accomplished	needed
worthy	exemplary	qualified	adequate
admirable	praiseworthy	efficient	ample
valuable	virtuous	reliable	healthy

antonyms: bad, terrible

GREAT *(great, greater, greatest)*

Meaning #1	**great** can mean *important*
	The Empire State building is *great*.
	The Empire State building is *impressive*.

Meaning #2	**great** can mean *excellent*
	It was a *great* movie.
	It was a *dynamite* movie.

Meaning #3	**great** can mean *large*
	The *great* pyramids rose up from the desert floor.
	The *massive* pyramids rose up from the desert floor.

A.	**B.**	**C.**
important	**excellent**	**large**
grand	best	big
extraordinary	perfect	enormous
glorious	terrific	huge
impressive	marvelous	immense
distinguished	supreme	vast
outstanding	fantastic	gigantic
remarkable	wonderful	jumbo
famous	exceptional	colossal
notable	tremendous	humongous
highly regarded	magnificent	mammoth
renowned	dynamite	massive

antonyms: poor, minor, small

HAPPY *(happy, happier, happiest)*

Meaning #1	happy means *glad*
	The *happy* audience applauded for over five minutes.
	The *exuberant* audience applauded for over five minutes.

A.	B.	C.
glad	**glad**	**glad**
pleased	overjoyed	radiant
cheerful	ecstatic	delighted
jolly	excited	lighthearted
joyful	thrilled	carefree
gleeful	lively	blessed
playful	exuberant	satisfied
merry	jubilant	content
jovial	blissful	gratified

antonym: sad

HARD *(hard, harder, hardest)*

Meaning #1	**hard** can mean *difficult*
	The hike to the mountain summit was *hard*.
	The hike to the mountain summit was *demanding*.

Meaning #2	**hard** can mean *rocklike*
	The granite kitchen counters are *hard*.
	The granite kitchen counters are *solid*.

A.	B.	C.
difficult	**difficult**	**rocklike**
tough	strenuous	rocky
rugged	rigorous	rigid
rough	laborious	stiff
complicated	tricky	firm
involved	demanding	dense
tiring	uphill	solid
exhausting	troublesome	strong
grueling	effortful	tough
weary	serious	unyielding

antonym: easy

(HEALTHY) *(healthy, health<u>ier</u>, health<u>iest</u>)*

Meaning #1	**healthy** can mean *not sick*
	As a result of diet and exercise, Marta is *healthy*.
	As a result of diet and exercise, Marta is *physically fit*.

Meaning #2	**healthy** can mean *wholesome*
	She eats *healthy* foods.
	She eats *nourishing* foods.

A.	**B.**	**C.**
not sick	**not sick**	**wholesome**
well	able-bodied	beneficial
all right	physically fit	health-giving
normal	active	healthful
strong	lively	nourishing
hardy	athletic	nutritious
sturdy	flourishing	unpolluted
trim	bright-eyed	disease-free
fit	rosy-cheeked	fresh

antonyms: sick, ill

HONEST *(honest, more honest, most honest)*

Meaning #1	**honest** means *fair*
	The *honest* store owner always had reasonable prices. The *reputable* store owner always had reasonable prices.

A.

fair

truthful
honorable
moral
ethical
trustworthy
law-abiding
scrupulous
straightforward

B.

fair

real
genuine
sincere
respectable
decent
earnest
reliable
reputable

antonyms: untruthful, sneaky, lying

HOT *(hot, hotter, hottest)*

Meaning #1	**hot** can mean *heated*
	The *hot* day forced the travelers to seek air-conditioned hotels. The *sweltering* day forced the travelers to seek air-conditioned hotels.

Meaning #2	**hot** can mean *spicy*
	The Mexican dish was too *hot* for me. The Mexican dish was too *peppery* for me.

A.	B.	C.
heated	**heated**	**spicy**
warm	boiling	peppery
burning	scalding	zesty
flaming	scorching	highly seasoned
fiery	tropical	sharp
blazing	steaming	pungent
sizzling	sweltering	biting
blistering	oppressive	fiery

antonym: cold

IMPORTANT *(important, more important, most important)*

Meaning #1	important means *great*
	The opening speech was made by an *important* woman.
	The opening speech was made by an *influential* woman.

A.

great

outstanding
remarkable
exceptional
momentous
extraordinary
magnificent
significant
notable

B.

great

critical
vital
urgent
crucial
necessary
essential
meaningful
relevant

C.

great

leading
well-known
famous
legendary
influential
powerful
distinguished
serious

antonyms: unimportant, irrelevant

INTERESTING *(interesting, more interesting, most interesting)*

Meaning #1	**interesting** means *fascinating*
	Michael couldn't lift his eyes from the *interesting* mystery.
	Michael couldn't lift his eyes from the *engrossing* mystery.

A.

fascinating

intriguing
thought-provoking
stimulating
unusual
curious
entertaining
inviting
amusing

antonyms: boring, uninteresting

B.

fascinating

attractive
appealing
pleasing
lovely
delightful
enchanting
impressive
exceptional

KIND *(kind, kind__er__, kind__est__)*

Meaning #1	**kind** means *helpful*
	The *kind* workers at the homeless shelter made everyone feel welcome.
	The *compassionate* workers at the homeless shelter made everyone feel welcome.

A.

helpful

friendly
thoughtful
understanding
considerate
sympathetic
humane
neighborly
good-hearted
gracious

antonyms: mean, unkind

B.

helpful

loving
affectionate
courteous
generous
charitable
gentle
sweet
tender
compassionate

LITTLE (little, littl*er*, littl*est*)

Meaning #1	**little** means *small*
	Nancy, though a fifth grader, is *little*.
	Nancy, though a fifth grader, is *petite*.

A.

small

tiny
teeny-weeny
short
petite
slight
dinky
undersized
undeveloped

antonym: big

B.

small

skinny
skimpy
young
brief
mini
miniature
microscopic
diminutive

C.

small

barely enough
few
meager
scant
paltry
measly
insufficient
scarce

LOUD *(loud, louder, loudest)*

Meaning #1	**loud** means *not quiet*
	The *loud* horn could be heard for miles.
	The *blaring* horn could be heard for miles.

A.

not quiet

noisy
booming
blaring
roaring
crashing
pealing
piercing

B.

not quiet

thundering
thunderous
jarring
harsh
ear-splitting
ear-piercing
loud-mouthed

C.

not quiet

deafening
resounding
rowdy
turbulent
clamorous
raucous
rambunctious

antonym: quiet

MAD *(mad, madd__er__, madd__est__)*

Meaning #1	**mad** can mean *angry*
	When his CDs were stolen, Marcus was *mad*.
	When his CDs were stolen, Marcus was *furious*.

Meaning #2	**mad** can mean *crazy*
	When her sister was killed, Patrice acted *mad*.
	When her sister was killed, Patrice acted *unstable*.

A.	**B.**	**C.**
angry	**angry**	**crazy**
very upset	irritated	insane
furious	irate	berserk
fuming	infuriated	deranged
cross	enraged	demented
uptight	ferocious	frenzied
bitter	distraught	raving
annoyed	exasperated	delirious
resentful	uncontrolled	unstable
ill-tempered	agitated	unhinged

antonyms: happy, unruffled, sane

MEAN (*mean, meaner, meanest*)

Meaning #1	**mean** means *cruel*
	The *mean* tiger kept all the zoo workers at a distance.
	The *vicious* tiger kept all the zoo workers at a distance.

A.

cruel

vicious
malicious
nasty
vile
dangerous
treacherous
abusive

antonym: kind

B.

cruel

unkind
unfriendly
rude
unpleasant
disagreeable
bad-tempered
cantankerous

C.

cruel

unfeeling
spiteful
lowdown
despicable
intolerable
unscrupulous
ruthless

NEAT *(neat, neater, neatest)*

Meaning #1	**neat** means *tidy*
	The *neat* bedroom shocked Pete's mother!
	The *orderly* bedroom shocked Pete's mother!

A.

tidy

orderly
organized
systematic
methodical
shipshape
well-kept
spotless

antonyms: untidy, messy

B.

tidy

immaculate
spick-and-span
clean-cut
dapper
well-groomed
fastidious
trim

NEW *(new, newer, newest)*

Meaning #1	**new** means *not old*
	The *new* manual contained information on caring for the Volkswagen.
	The *up-to-date* manual contained information on caring for the Volkswagen.

A.

not old

fresh
young
contemporary
current
up-to-date
latest
improved
recent

B.

not old

modern
cutting-edge
newfangled
original
unused
unknown
distinct
unfamiliar

antonym: old

NICE *(nice, nicer, nicest)*

Meaning #1	**nice** means *pleasant*
	The *nice* teacher assisted the students.
	The *considerate* teacher assisted the students.

A.

pleasant

fine
pleasing
sweet
friendly
delightful
charming
groovy
nifty
great
superior

B.

pleasant

lovely
attractive
striking
eye-catching
kind
polite
courteous
considerate
well-mannered
gracious

C.

pleasant

agreeable
approved
admirable
likeable
favorable
enjoyable
inviting
tasteful
proper
decent

antonyms: mean, unpleasant

OLD (*old, older, oldest*)

Meaning #1	**old** means *aged*
	The *old* man surprised the children with his witty comments.
	The *elderly* man surprised the children with his witty comments.

A.

aged

elderly
aging
long-lived
veteran
senior
mature
experienced
seasoned

B.

aged

time-honored
venerable
immortal
ancient
worn-out
broken-down
decayed
decrepit

C.

aged

previous
former
antique
vintage
outdated
obsolete
antiquated
primitive

antonyms: new, young

PERFECT *(perfect, more perfect, most perfect)*

Meaning #1	**perfect** means *flawless*
	The quilt, though made in 1895, is *perfect*.
	The quilt, though made in 1895, is *unblemished*.

A.

flawless

faultless
accurate
correct
complete
intact
ideal
best
superb
splendid

antonyms: flawed, faulty

B.

flawless

supreme
excellent
greatest
spotless
unblemished
unequaled
unbroken
undamaged
unimpaired

PRETTY *(pretty, prettier, prettiest)*

Meaning #1	**pretty** means *good-looking*
	The red and orange sunset was *pretty*.
	The red and orange sunset was *exquisite*.

A.

good-looking

attractive
beautiful
handsome
dazzling
stunning
magnificent
glamorous
gorgeous
elegant

B.

good-looking

adorable
delicate
dainty
graceful
marvelous
radiant
charming
exquisite
captivating

C.

good-looking

excellent
splendid
appealing
tasteful
cute
darling
lovely
pleasant
fair

antonyms: unattractive, ugly

QUIET *(quiet, more quiet, most quiet)*

Meaning #1	quiet can mean *not loud*
	The class could not hear Erin's voice because it was so *quiet*.
	The class could not hear Erin's voice because it was so *soft*.

Meaning #2	quiet can mean *calm*
	Nothing could disturb the *quiet* Sunday afternoon.
	Nothing could disturb the *tranquil* Sunday afternoon.

A.

not loud

silent
soundless
noiseless
speechless
mute
still
hushed
soft

antonym: noisy

B.

not loud

muffled
unspeaking
inaudible
secretive
tight-lipped
clammed up
close-mouthed
uncommunicative

C.

calm

restful
easy
peaceful
serene
slow
mellow
unruffled
tranquil

SAD *(sad, sadder, saddest)*

Meaning #1	**sad** means *unhappy*
	Grace was *sad* when her cat disappeared.
	Grace was *forlorn* when her cat disappeared.

A.

unhappy

glum
low
blue
gloomy
dismal
dreary
pitiful
hurting
hopeless
dejected
melancholy

antonym: happy

B.

unhappy

miserable
pathetic
depressed
depressing
disheartened
dissatisfied
displeased
discontented
unfortunate
upsetting
regretful

C.

unhappy

grieving
mournful
sorrowful
heartsick
heartbroken
tearful
discouraged
pessimistic
despondent
despairing
forlorn

SCARED *(scared, more scared, most scared)*

Meaning #1	scared means *afraid*
	Franco was *scared* as he readied himself for his first airplane jump.
	Franco was *apprehensive* as he readied himself for his first airplane jump.

A.

afraid

terrified
frightened
fearful
alarmed
suppressed
startled
spooked
panicked

B.

afraid

terror-stricken
panic-stricken
petrified
disturbed
upset
distressed
dismayed
nervous

C.

afraid

anxious
worried
apprehensive
concerned
uneasy
reluctant
hesitant
cautious

antonym: unafraid

SHY *(shy, shier, shiest)*

Meaning #1	shy means *bashful*
	The *shy* child opened the door to the classroom cautiously.
	The *timid* child opened the door to the classroom cautiously.

A.

bashful

timid
quiet
introverted
reserved
retiring
modest
fearful
afraid

B.

bashful

cautious
hesitant
reluctant
humble
nervous
distrustful
suspicious
apprehensive

antonyms: bold, confident

SICK *(sick, sicker, sickest)*

Meaning #1	sick means *ill*
	After eating ALL of the candy, Lucas was *sick*.
	After eating ALL of the candy, Lucas was *nauseated*.

A.

ill

unwell
unhealthy
diseased
indisposed
carsick
seasick
airsick

antonym: healthy

B.

ill

weak
frail
suffering
ailing
out of sorts
under the weather
laid up

C.

ill

infected
feverish
nauseated
queasy
bedridden
impaired
incurable

(**SKINNY**) *(skinny, skinni<u>er</u>, skinni<u>est</u>)*

Meaning #1	skinny means *not fat*
	The sixth grade twins are tall and *skinny*.
	The sixth grade twins are tall and *lanky*.

A.

not fat

scrawny
thin
slender
slight
lean
bony
spindly
lanky

antonym: fat

B.

not fat

wiry
frail
malnourished
undernourished
underweight
emaciated
skeletal
gaunt

SMART *(smart, smarter, smartest)*

Meaning #1	smart means *intelligent*
	I knew Michael was *smart* when I viewed his science fair project.
	I knew Michael was *ingenious* when I viewed his science fair project.

A.

intelligent

bright
brilliant
sharp
brainy
genius
ingenious
talented
gifted

B.

intelligent

sensible
wise
astute
skilled
adept
effective
resourceful
alert

C.

intelligent

quick
clever
keen
witty
quick-witted
shrewd
crafty
cunning

antonym: dumb

STRONG *(strong, strong**er**, strong**est**)*

Meaning #1	strong can mean *powerful—physically*
	As a result of visiting the gym daily, Mary is *strong*.
	As a result of visiting the gym daily, Mary is *muscular*.

Meaning #2	strong can mean *determined—mentally*
	The *strong* governor would not change his ideas.
	The *uncompromising* governor would not change his ideas.

A.
powerful—physically

husky
muscular
sturdy
well-built
firm
athletic

antonym: weak

B.
powerful—physically

brawny
mighty
forceful
able-bodied
robust
vigorous

C.
determined—mentally

serious
courageous
aggressive
intense
uncompromising
steadfast

STUPID *(stupid, stupider, stupidest)*

Meaning #1	**stupid** means *dumb*
	The principal was tired of the *stupid* pranks.
	The principal was tired of the *senseless* pranks.

A.

dumb

dull
unintelligent
naive
unthinking
dense
thoughtless
absentminded

antonym: smart

B.

dumb

foolish
foolhardy
unwise
irresponsible
childish
silly
reckless

C.

dumb

senseless
brainless
mindless
pointless
meaningless
irrelevant
shortsighted

TERRIBLE *(terrible, more terrible, most terrible)*

Meaning #1	**terrible** means *awful*
	The *terrible* train wreck caused many deaths.
	The *disastrous* train wreck caused many deaths.

A.

awful

bad
horrible
horrid
lousy
dreadful
horrendous
horrifying
frightening

B.

awful

gruesome
repulsive
monstrous
hideous
ghastly
atrocious
evil
vile

C.

awful

disastrous
dangerous
revolting
shocking
appalling
disturbing
unacceptable
unfortunate

antonym: wonderful

TIRED *(tired, more tired, most tired)*

Meaning #1	**tired** means *sleepy*
	The *tired* student's head bobbed up and down in class.
	The *weary* student's head bobbed up and down in class.

A.

sleepy

weary
fatigued
worn-out
tuckered out
burned out
done in
droopy
drowsy
sluggish

antonym: energized

B.

sleepy

drained
beat
listless
weak
bored
blasé
haggard
distressed
fed up

UGLY (ugly, uglier, ugliest)

Meaning #1	ugly can mean *unattractive*
	Jonathan looked *ugly* in the monster costume and makeup.
	Jonathan looked *hideous* in the monster costume and makeup.

Meaning #2	ugly can mean *disgusting*
	The photos of the battle were so *ugly* that many observers glanced away.
	The photos of the battle were so *revolting* that many observers glanced away.

A. unattractive	B. unattractive	C. disgusting
awful	grungy	disagreeable
gross	unsightly	sickening
plain	unbecoming	appalling
homely	unseemly	loathsome
bad-looking	monstrous	repulsive
grotesque	abominable	repelling
grisly	nasty	revolting
frightful	unlovely	despicable
hideous	undesirable	repugnant

antonyms: beautiful, lovely

(WEAK) *(weak, weaker, weakest)*

Meaning #1	**weak** can mean *not strong*
	The *weak* boy could not lift himself out of the wheelchair.
	The *frail* boy could not lift himself out of the wheelchair.

Meaning #2	**weak** can mean *cowardly*
	Many of the *weak* children resisted going into the bat-filled cave.
	Many of the *insecure* children resisted going into the bat-filled cave.

Meaning #3	**weak** can mean *dim*
	The light was so *weak* that we could not read.
	The light was so *faint* that we could not read.

Meaning #4	**weak** can mean *inadequate*
	The ideas presented in the paper were *weak*.
	The ideas presented in the paper were *unconvincing*.

A.	B.	C.	D.
not strong	**cowardly**	**dim**	**inadequate**
fragile	frightened	dull	faulty
puny	nervous	low	lacking
sickly	uncertain	poor	limited
shaky	insecure	pale	incomplete
delicate	hesitant	quiet	incompetent
feeble	gutless	soft	ineffective
frail	spineless	faint	substandard
limp	fainthearted	gentle	unsatisfactory
unsteady	powerless	distant	unconvincing
flimsy	sissy	indistinct	invalid
wobbly	pathetic	imperceptible	immature

antonyms: strong, brave, capable

WEIRD (*weird, weirder, weirdest*)

Meaning #1	**weird** means *strange*
	The purple mansion with orange trim and a peaked roof is *weird*. The purple mansion with orange trim and a peaked roof is *outlandish*.

A.

strange
odd
unusual
peculiar
bizarre
different
irregular
unnatural
supernatural

B.

strange
uncommon
unconventional
abnormal
outlandish
ridiculous
absurd
mysterious
curious

C.

strange
crazy
kooky
offbeat
screwy
eccentric
spooky
eerie
creepy

antonyms: normal, usual

(WILD) *(wild, wilder, wildest)*

Meaning #1	**wild** can mean *disorderly*
	After recess, the sixth graders were *wild*.
	After recess, the sixth graders were *rowdy*.

Meaning #2	**wild** can mean *untamed*
	Animals found in the jungles are *wild*.
	Animals found in the jungles are *undomesticated*.

A.	B.	C.
disorderly	**disorderly**	**untamed**
rowdy	berserk	unbroken
boisterous	crazy	undomesticated
uncontrolled	foolish	uncivilized
noisy	agitated	primitive
uproarious	unmanageable	barbaric
hysterical	uproarious	ferocious
frantic	impetuous	savage

antonyms: calm, tame

WONDERFUL *(wonderful, more wonderful, most wonderful)*

Meaning #1	**wonderful** means *terrific*
	The *wonderful* statue rose two stories above the earth.
	The *astonishing* statue rose two stories above the earth.

A.

terrific

great
fine
super
excellent
amazing
astonishing
fabulous
fantastic
enjoyable
tremendous

B.

terrific

splendid
superb
incredible
exceptional
sensational
extraordinary
phenomenal
fascinating
marvelous
staggering

C.

terrific

miraculous
glorious
spectacular
magnificent
astounding
remarkable
awesome
awe-inspiring
outstanding
stupendous

antonym: terrible

YOUNG *(young, younger, youngest)*

Meaning #1	**young** means *not old*
	The *young* colt struggled to stand.
	The *fledgling* colt struggled to stand.

A.

not old

youthful
childish
juvenile
immature
inexperienced
little
new
fledgling

antonyms: old, mature

B.

not old

fresh
early
recent
modern
unfinished
undeveloped
developing
unseasoned

BUILDINGS

Synonyms	structures dwellings	architecture constructions	residences housing

A.
housing (single family)
dwellings
homes
trailers
mobile homes
bungalows
cabins
huts
shacks
apartments
flats

B.
housing (single family)
castles
mansions
villas
plantations
manors
haciendas
chateaus
igloos
houseboats
tents

C.
housing (multiple family)
duplexes
apartment buildings
condominiums
town houses
tenements
dormitories
barracks
trailer parks
hi-rises
quarters

D.
buildings (retail)
restaurants
grocery stores
drug stores
shoe stores
department stores
convenience stores
discount stores
clothing stores
electronics stores
gas stations
fast food restaurants
office supply stores
movie theaters
music stores
hair salons

E.
buildings (service)
hospitals
banks
libraries
fire stations
police stations
post offices
city halls
hotels
dentist's offices
doctor's offices
churches
synagogues
mosques
convention centers
auditoriums

F.
rooms
spaces
bedrooms
living rooms
dining rooms
family rooms
dens
kitchens
lofts
garages
hallways
attics
basements
home offices
rec rooms
gyms

CLOTHES

Synonyms	clothing	garments	wardrobe
	apparel	costumes	outfits

A.
shirts

T-shirts
blouses
tops
sweaters
pullovers
vests
sweatshirts
tank tops
turtlenecks
jerseys

B.
pants

slacks
trousers
jeans
shorts
cutoffs
tights
Capri pants
bell-bottoms
dungarees
overalls

C.
shoes

sandals
boots
sneakers
heels
slippers
moccasins
flip-flops
pumps
flats
slip-ons

D.
skirts and dresses

jumpers
skirts
formals
slips
wedding dresses

E.
coats

jackets
raincoats
overcoats
windbreakers
parkas

F.
shawls

capes
stoles
serapes
cloaks
ponchos

EVENTS

Synonyms	occurrences	occasions	incidents
	happenings	experiences	episodes

A.
beginnings (of events)

starts
onsets
starting points
origins
births
openings
inceptions
kickoffs
initiatives
commencements
inaugurations
emergence

B.
endings (of events)

finishes
completions
conclusions
results
finales
windups
culminations
closings
finish lines
terminations
wrap-ups

C.
disasters

accidents
wrecks
catastrophes
calamities
fiascoes
debacles
devastations
tragedies
misfortunes
setbacks
emergencies
collapses
hazards

D.
celebrations

parties
festivals
galas
feasts
occasions
holidays
ceremonies
commemorations
rituals
anniversaries
jubilees
festivities
wingdings

E.
entertainment

games
play
fun
recreation
pastimes
relaxation
amusements
performances
sports
picnics
hobbies
avocations
leisure activities

F.
specific events

parades
circuses
county fairs
birthday parties
bar mitzvahs
bat mitzvahs
engagement parties
plays
weddings
ballgames
street fairs
bazaars
baby showers
concerts
grand openings

FEELINGS

| **Synonyms** | emotions | sensations | impressions |
| | intuitions | ideas | senses |

A.
words for happiness

gladness
delight
joy
satisfaction
bliss
contentment
enjoyment
excitement
elation
cheer
merriment
joviality
exuberance
gaiety

B.
words for sadness

unhappiness
sorrow
misery
depression
grief
heartache
suffering
anguish
agony
disappointment
gloom
melancholy
doldrums
discontentment

C.
words for love

affection
passion
devotion
allegiance
dedication
fondness
admiration
adoration
appreciation
friendship
tenderness
faithfulness
enchantment
infatuation

D.
words for excitement

interest
eagerness
enthusiasm
exuberance
vigor
passion
conviction
zeal
joy
exhilaration
elation
devotion
fanaticism
fervor

E.
words for anger

rage
outrage
infuriation
fury
temper
hatred
animosity
resentment
antagonism
dislike
irritation
disdain
bitterness
displeasure

F.
words for peace

calm
calmness
quiet
stillness
comfort
serenity
tranquility
contentment
placidity
quietude
pacifism
conciliation

Nouns

words for people, places, things, and ideas

OUTDOOR PLACES

Synonyms	destinations settings	scenes sites	locations spots

A.
places where you drive

streets
roads
highways
avenues
boulevards
lanes
turnpikes
parkways

B.
places with grass

yards
parks
fields
meadows
prairies
pastures
grasslands
plains

C.
land forms

hills
mountains
buttes
mounds
valleys
gorges
canyons
ravines
gullies
gulches
arroyos

D.
places with trees

woods
forests
woodlands
wilds
jungles
parks
orchards
farms

E.
bodies of water

rivers
streams
brooks
creeks
canals
lakes
ponds
estuaries

F.
bodies of water

oceans
seas
inlets
bays
coves
lagoons
straits
everglades

PEOPLE

Synonyms	persons	humans	individuals
	human beings	men and women	population

A.

group of people

crowd
mob
throng
swarm
horde
gathering
collection
congregation
assembly
team
multitude

B.

people who like each other/people who know each other

friends
amigos
partners
pals
allies
buddies
comrades
mates
acquaintances
companions
colleagues

C.

people who dislike each other/people who fight each other

enemies
opponents
foes
rivals
attackers
assailants
adversaries
antagonists

D.

people who know a lot/ people who really like something

experts
authorities
specialists
masters
professionals
enthusiasts
fanatics
devotees
diehards
aficionados
connoisseurs

E.

people who are young

children
youngsters
offspring
babies
infants
toddlers
tots
kids
teenagers
descendants
heirs

F.

people who compete/ people who win

athletes
competitors
challengers
rivals
candidates
contestants
winners
champions
opponents
contenders
aspirants

THINGS

Synonyms	objects articles	items belongings	possessions gadgets

A.

food

groceries
cuisines
provisions
meals
grub
chow
snacks
foodstuffs
sustenance
nourishment
vittles
edibles

B.

money

cash
currency
change
coins
funds
wealth
loot
greenbacks
petty cash
loose change

C.

businesses

companies
firms
corporations
stores
organizations
establishments
partnerships
cartels

D.

furniture

chairs
sofas
couches
loveseats
seats
benches
tables
desks
nightstands
dressers
beds
shelves
bookcases

E.

jewelry

necklaces
pendants
bracelets
earrings
rings
charms
watches
pins
brooches
anklets
stickpins
nose rings

F.

printed material

books
paperbacks
hardbacks
texts
publications
newspapers
magazines
journals
catalogues
directories

THINGS PEOPLE MAKE

Synonyms	products creations inventions productions works of art

A.
music

songs
compositions
scores
tunes
melodies
symphonies
ballads
harmonies
spirituals
lullabies
operas
overtures
soundtracks
ditties

B.
art

paintings
drawings
illustrations
sketches
doodles
etchings
cartoons
photographs
sculptures
crafts
watercolors

C.
stories

novels
short stories
tales
fairy tales
tall tales
myths
mysteries
fiction
narratives
accounts
novellas

D.
shows

plays
performances
productions
pageants
spectacles
happenings
movies
videos
concerts
readings

E.
gardens

vegetable gardens
flower gardens
yards
garden patches
borders
landscapes
scenery
parks

F.
meals

breakfasts
brunches
lunches
dinners
suppers
feasts
banquets
desserts
snacks

VEHICLES

| Synonyms | carriers | transporters | conveyances |

A.
cars

sedans
station wagons
convertibles
sports cars
jeeps
economy cars
hybrids
SUVs
minivans

B.
boats

ships
cruise ships
ferries
yachts
rowboats
canoes
kayaks

C.
trucks

pickups
vans
eighteen-wheelers
trailer-trucks
semis
delivery trucks

D.
aircraft

airplanes
jets
helicopters
gliders
crop dusters

E.
trains

railroad cars
rails
subways
trams
boxcars
engines
light rails

F.
other vehicles

bicycles
wagons
motorcycles
scooters
skateboards
roller skates
wheelbarrows

WORKERS

Synonyms	employees educators	service providers professionals	technicians artists

A.

transportation workers

airline pilot
bus driver
taxi driver
train engineer
conductor
engineer
flight attendant
limousine driver

B.

government workers

city manager
police captain
police officer
fire captain
firefighter
post office
    supervisor
postal worker
judge
district attorney
social worker
garbage collector

C.

building trade workers

roofer
plumber
carpenter
electrician
mechanic
architect
painter
contractor

D.

business workers

CEO
manager
supervisor
sales
    representative
accountant
human resource
    manager
receptionist
secretary

E.

school workers

principal
office manager
teacher
speech therapist
band director
librarian
custodian
secretary
school nurse
crossing guard

F.

personal service workers

barber
hairdresser
hairstylist
jeweler
dressmaker
tailor
shoe-repair
    person
manicurist

G.

health workers

doctor
surgeon
nurse
dietitian
nutritionist
dentist
dental hygienist
lab technician
physical therapist
personal trainer

H.

technology workers

programmer
technician
graphic designer
computer
    engineer
Webmaster
data entry person

BUILD

Present tense	Past tense
build	**built**
make	made
create	created
fashion	fashioned
construct	constructed
develop	developed
put together	put together
assemble	assembled
produce	produced
manufacture	manufactured
form	formed
craft	crafted
design	designed
engineer	engineered

antonyms: destroy, tear down, take apart

COME

Present tense	Past tense
come	**came**
arrive	arrived
show up	showed up
appear	appeared
enter	entered
approach	approached
visit	visited
check in	checked in
clock in	clocked in
reach	reached
pop in	popped in
turn up	turned up

antonyms: go

EAT

Present tense	Past tense
eat	**ate**
feed	fed
dine	dined
feast	feasted
snack	snacked
nibble	nibbled
gobble	gobbled
bite	bit
chew	chewed
digest	digested
swallow	swallowed
ingest	ingested
munch	munched
gulp	gulped
devour	devoured
consume	consumed

antonym: fast, starve

FIND

Present tense	Past tense
find	**found**
discover	discovered
detect	detected
spot	spotted
locate	located
run across	ran across
pinpoint	pinpointed
identify	identified
uncover	uncovered
acquire	acquired
encounter	encountered
obtain	obtained
unearth	unearthed

antonym: lose

GET

Present tense	Past tense
get	**got**
obtain	obtained
acquire	acquired
receive	received
gain	gained
attain	attained
buy	bought
capture	captured
inherit	inherited
take	took
catch	caught
extract	extracted
glean	gleaned
earn	earned
elicit	elicited
recover	recovered
retrieve	retrieved
fetch	fetched

antonyms: lose, give

GIVE

Present tense	Past tense
give	**gave**
present	presented
donate	donated
contribute	contributed
offer	offered
award	awarded
hand over	handed over
entrust	entrusted
provide	provided
dispense	dispensed
deliver	delivered
pay	paid
remit	remitted
pass down	passed down
bestow	bestowed
bequeath	bequeathed
endow	endowed
confer	conferred

antonyms: take

GO

Present tense	Past tense
go	**went**
move toward	moved toward
ride	rode
travel	traveled
pass	passed
proceed	proceeded
head	headed
visit	visited
leave	left
depart	departed
exit	exited
disappear	disappeared
stray	strayed
wander	wandered
roam	roamed
rove	roved
ramble	rambled
gallivant	gallivanted
withdraw	withdrew
retreat	retreated
hurry	hurried
fly	flew
flee	fled
escape	escaped
abscond	absconded

antonyms: come, appear

GROW

Present tense	Past tense
grow	**grew**
expand	expanded
increase	increased
multiply	multiplied
enlarge	enlarged
develop	developed
mature	matured
ripen	ripened
sprout	sprouted
flourish	flourished
thrive	thrived
compile	compiled
accrue	accrued
inflate	inflated
magnify	magnified
amplify	amplified
evolve	evolved

antonym: decrease, die

HAVE

Present tense	*Past tense*
have	**had**
possess	possessed
own	owned
keep	kept
retain	retained
hold	held
include	included
contain	contained
acquire	acquired
procure	procured
occupy	occupied

antonym: lose

HELP

Present tense	*Past tense*
help	**helped**
assist	assisted
lend a hand	lent a hand
aid	aided
serve	served
support	supported
back	backed
collaborate with	collaborated with
rescue	rescued
save	saved
nurture	nurtured
promote	promoted
stand behind	stood behind
endorse	endorsed

antonyms: hinder, prevent

KNOW

Present tense	Past tense
know	**knew**
understand	understood
comprehend	comprehended
grasp	grasped
realize	realized
perceive	perceived
recognize	recognized
acknowledge	acknowledged
appreciate	appreciated
[is] acquainted with	[was] acquainted with
[is] aware of	[was] aware of
[is] familiar with	[was] familiar with
[is] cognizant of	[was] cognizant of
[is] informed	[was] informed
distinguish	distinguished
discern	discerned

antonym: [is] ignorant

LET

Present tense	Past tense
let	**let**
allow	allowed
permit	permitted
authorize	authorized
sanction	sanctioned
agree	agreed
grant	granted
approve	approved
consent to	consented to
concede	conceded
enable	enabled
recommend	recommended
endorse	endorsed
put up with	put up with
tolerate	tolerated

antonyms: forbid, prevent

LIKE

Present tense	Past tense
like	**liked**
enjoy	enjoyed
love	loved
find appealing	found appealing
appreciate	appreciated
approve	approved
admire	admired
prize	prized
cherish	cherished
adore	adored
prefer	preferred
fancy	fancied
relish	relished
care for	cared for
care about	cared about
[is] fond of	[was] fond of
hold dear	held dear

antonym: dislike

LIVE

Present tense	Past tense
live	**lived**
exist	existed
dwell	dwelled
reside	resided
stay	stayed
settle	settled
continue	continued
survive	survived
inhabit	inhabited
occupy	occupied
abide	abided

antonyms: die, perish

MAKE

Present tense	*Past tense*
make	**made**
build	built
construct	constructed
prepare	prepared
produce	produced
manufacture	manufactured
form	formed
shape	shaped
create	created
invent	invented
generate	generated
compose	composed
put together	put together
assemble	assembled
synthesize	synthesized
accomplish	accomplished
fashion	fashioned

antonyms: destroy, take apart

PUT

Present tense	*Past tense*
put	**put**
set	set
place	placed
lay	laid
deposit	deposited
position	positioned
situate	situated
locate	located
park	parked
plunk	plunked
return	returned
replace	replaced
restore	restored
install	installed
rivet	riveted

antonyms: take, lift, remove

RUN

Present tense	*Past tense*
run	**ran**
jog	jogged
sprint	sprinted
hurry	hurried
rush	rushed
scamper	scampered
scurry	scurried
dash	dashed
dart	darted
race	raced
escape	escaped
flee	fled
trot	trotted
gallop	galloped
amble	ambled
lope	loped
bound	bounded

antonym: stand still

SAY

Present tense	*Past tense*
say	**said**
ask	asked
speak	spoke
tell	told
state	stated
declare	declared
announce	announced
pronounce	pronounced
voice	voiced
verbalize	verbalized
report	reported
disclose	disclosed
divulge	divulged
convey	conveyed
recite	recited
claim	claimed
allege	alleged
shout	shouted
exclaim	exclaimed
whisper	whispered
utter	uttered
remark	remarked
comment	commented
mention	mentioned

antonym: [is] quiet

SEE

Present tense	*Past tense*
see—look at	**saw—looked at**
observe	observed
view	viewed
notice	noticed
witness	witnessed
spot	spotted
glimpse	glimpsed
watch	watched
stare at	stared at
glare	glared
gaze	gazed
gawk	gawked
peer	peered
examine	examined
inspect	inspected
scan	scanned
survey	surveyed

antonyms: overlook, ignore

STAY

Present tense	*Past tense*
stay	**stayed**
remain	remained
wait	waited
linger	lingered
loiter	loitered
stick around	stuck around
hang out	hung out
hang around	hung around
persist	persisted
endure	endured
continue	continued
keep on	kept on

antonym: go

TAKE

Present tense	*Past tense*
take (1)	**took**
obtain	obtained
attain	attained
catch	caught
capture	captured
acquire	acquired
accept	accepted
seize	seized
confiscate	confiscated
collect	collected
steal	stole
grab	grabbed
snatch	snatched
apprehend	apprehended
ensnare	ensnared

antonym: give

Present tense	*Past tense*
take (2)	**took**
carry	carried
bring	brought
move	moved
transfer	transferred
relocate	relocated
transport	transported
bear	bore
haul	hauled
tote	toted
fetch	fetched
hoist	hoisted

antonym: not move

TALK

Present tense	*Past tense*
talk	**talked**
talk about	talked about
talk to	talked to
speak	spoke
converse	conversed
discuss	discussed
argue	argued
negotiate	negotiated
communicate	communicated
share	shared
consult	consulted
lecture	lectured
preach	preached
whisper	whispered
chat	chatted
chitchat	chitchatted
babble	babbled
blab	blabbed
report	reported
gossip	gossiped
rap	rapped

antonym: [is] quiet

THINK

Present tense	*Past tense*
think	**thought**
think about	thought about
imagine	imagined
believe	believed
assume	assumed
suppose	supposed
presume	presumed
consider	considered
ponder	pondered
meditate	meditated
reason	reasoned
deduce	deduced
understand	understood
comprehend	comprehended
reflect	reflected
contemplate	contemplated
picture	pictured
visualize	visualized
speculate	speculated
concentrate	concentrated
use [your] head	used [your] head
worry	worried
muse	mused
ruminate	ruminated

antonym: not ponder

USE

Present tense	*Past tense*
use (1)	**used (1)**
utilize	utilized
work with	worked with
employ	employed
finish with	finished with
operate	operated
make do	made do
make the most of	made the most of

antonym: not use

Present tense	*Past tense*
use up (2)	**used up (2)**
run out	ran out
waste	wasted
deplete	depleted
exhaust	exhausted
empty	emptied
drain	drained
wear [it] out	wore [it] out
lessen	lessened
finish	finished

antonym: not run out

WALK

Present tense	Past tense
walk	**walked**
move	moved
stroll	strolled
amble	ambled
saunter	sauntered
pace	paced
wander	wandered
meander	meandered
roam	roamed
shuffle	shuffled
dawdle	dawdled
trudge	trudged
march	marched
patrol	patrolled
hike	hiked
trek	trekked
step	stepped
stride	strode
tread	treaded

antonym: stand still

WANT

Present tense	Past tense
want	**wanted**
wish for	wished for
desire	desired
long for	longed for
hope for	hoped for
dream of	dreamed of
pine for	pined for
ache for	ached for
crave	craved
yearn	yearned
choose	chose
prefer	preferred
need	needed
require	required

antonym: not wish for

A.

ran ...

fast
quickly
rapidly
swiftly
eagerly
slowly
leisurely
lazily
easily
gracefully
smoothly
athletically
victoriously
jubilantly
triumphantly
awkwardly
unsteadily

B.

talked ...

kindly
softly
quietly
tenderly
pleasantly
patiently
calmly
hopefully
loudly
angrily
madly
harshly
abusively
excitedly
enthusiastically
admiringly
passionately
reasonably
candidly
honestly
persuasively
adamantly

C.

worked ...

hard
carefully
purposefully
responsibly
diligently
skillfully
productively
ardently
frantically
unrelentingly
independently
enthusiastically
industriously
voluntarily
slowly
quickly
carelessly
lazily
grudgingly
proudly
gladly
blissfully
cooperatively

D.

walked ...

slowly
shyly
gingerly
haltingly
silently
softly
stiffly
nervously
hesitantly
carefully
casually
painfully
expectantly
deliberately
determinedly
purposefully
courageously
boldly
proudly
gracefully
quickly
rapidly
fast

A.

sang …

well
sweetly
beautifully
pleasantly
harmoniously
gloriously
enthusiastically
fearlessly
angelically
wonderfully
joyfully
gaily
gleefully
blissfully
terribly
raucously
shakily
hoarsely
breathlessly
reluctantly
timidly

B.

argued …

fairly
respectfully
reasonably
cleverly
calmly
politely
seriously
pointedly
firmly
frankly
loudly
forcefully
passionately
arrogantly
fiercely
ferociously
vehemently
rudely
provocatively
convincingly

C.

acted …

positively
brilliantly
cleverly
generously
pleasantly
bravely
courageously
valiantly
nobly
gallantly
peacefully
righteously
negatively
stupidly
cowardly
thoughtlessly
absurdly
playfully
innocently
shyly
quickly
frantically
wildly
poorly

D.

gave …

generously
graciously
responsibly
caringly
lovingly
thoughtfully
selflessly
respectfully
confidently
carefully
prudently
supportively
sympathetically
philanthropically
altruistically
eagerly
selfishly
stingily
hesitantly
reluctantly
regretfully
imprudently
apprehensively
accidentally
secretively
anonymously

A.

behaved …

well
masterfully
expertly
appropriately
lovingly
honorably
wisely
thoughtfully
carefully
deliberately
bravely
politely
piously
poorly
rudely
crudely
offensively
dishonestly
dangerously
emotionally
naturally

B.

laughed …

hard
loudly
wholeheartedly
exuberantly
joyfully
hilariously
hysterically
deliriously
jokingly
jovially
comically
amusingly
playfully
mischievously
gently
amiably
rudely
snidely
insincerely

C.

spoke …

fast
slowly
politely
respectfully
favorably
comfortingly
honestly
earnestly
appropriately
tactfully
apologetically
persuasively
exuberantly
jokingly
casually
rudely
conceitedly
accusingly
arrogantly
brashly
bluntly
dishonestly
untruthfully
emotionally
tearfully
shyly
sheepishly

D.

typed …

fast
quickly
rapidly
furiously
relentlessly
skillfully
expertly
automatically
dexterously
adroitly
rhythmically
carefully
accurately
perfectly
precisely
inaccurately
thoughtlessly
clumsily
awkwardly
poorly
ineptly
slowly

Adverbs
words that tell "how"

A.

responded ...

quickly
immediately
instantly
positively
carefully
accurately
thoughtfully
honestly
enthusiastically
exuberantly
eagerly
confidently
convincingly
negatively
poorly
halfheartedly
insincerely
rudely
sarcastically
joyfully

B.

cheered ...

loudly
noisily
uproariously
enthusiastically
hysterically
passionately
emotionally
exuberantly
wildly
boisterously
rambunctiously
riotously
unrestrainedly
frantically
approvingly
reluctantly
responsively

C.

prayed ...

quietly
silently
peacefully
religiously
reverently
piously
solemnly
humbly
devotedly
earnestly
faithfully
patiently
hopefully
thoughtfully
contemplatively
reflectively
sorrowfully
mournfully
boastfully
proudly

D.

wrote ...

well
brilliantly
elegantly
excellently
masterfully
artfully
positively
constructively
clearly
concisely
accurately
expressively
effortlessly
diligently
vividly
believably
confidently
compellingly
emotionally
nostalgically
pretentiously
frequently
prolifically
poorly
unclearly
allusively
disparagingly

A.

shared ...

generously
joyfully
happily
openheartedly
wholeheartedly
easily
eagerly
enthusiastically
magnanimously
thoughtfully
sympathetically
empathetically
charitably
altruistically
reluctantly
stingily

B.

waited ...

calmly
patiently
silently
quietly
dutifully
obediently
loyally
faithfully
unwaveringly
observantly
watchfully
hopefully
longingly
alertly
expectantly
anxiously
fearfully
impatiently
restlessly
nonchalantly
stubbornly

C.

answered ...

correctly
accurately
exactly
thoroughly
completely
thoughtfully
impartially
honestly
truthfully
carefully
methodically
confidently
irrefutably
directly
candidly
eagerly
enthusiastically
spontaneously
agreeably
negatively
incorrectly
wrongly
indifferently
apathetically
foolishly
anxiously
disapprovingly
angrily
aggressively
defiantly

D.

moved ...

fast
quickly
rapidly
swiftly
suddenly
abruptly
unexpectedly
immediately
hurriedly
hastily
sprightly
energetically
easily
nimbly
spryly
gracefully
athletically
carefully
busily
restlessly
awkwardly
clumsily
stiffly
slowly
gingerly
haltingly

Where and When
words and phrases

Where Words	here	there	somewhere	anywhere
	nowhere	inside	outside	nearby

Where Phrase	Example	Where Phrase	Example
above …	above the table	near …	near the mall
across …	across the street	next to …	next to the market
against …	against the wall	on …	on the carpet
around …	around the corner	out of …	out of the box
at …	at the mountain peak	outside …	outside the pool
behind …	behind the chair	over …	over the soiled couch
below …	below the window	through …	through the gate
beneath …	beneath the balcony	throughout …	throughout the field
beside …	beside the garage	to..	to the dock
between …	between the houses	toward …	toward the entrance
beyond …	beyond the fence	under …	under the water
by …	by the lake	up …	up the ladder
down …	down the road	upon …	upon the counter
in …	in the attic	in front of …	in front of the car
inside …	inside the cabin	in back of …	in back of the school
into …	into the living room		

Where and When
words and phrases

When Words	then	now	later
	yesterday	today	tomorrow

Use these words with the following times.	this	next	last
	every	some	

Times of Day	Days	Holidays (examples)	Months		Seasons
morning	Sunday	New Years Day	January	July	Fall
noon	Monday	Valentine's Day	February	August	Winter
afternoon	Tuesday	Easter	March	September	Spring
evening	Wednesday	Memorial Day	April	October	Summer
night	Thursday	Labor Day	May	November	
	Friday	Christmas	June	December	
	Saturday	Hanukkah			

When Phrase	Example	When Phrase	Example
after …	after school	in …	in the late afternoon
about …	about four o'clock	on …	on a summer day
around …	around noon	since …	since the hurricane
before …	before Christmas	until …	until we finish
by …	by the deadline	while …	while everyone studied
during …	during March		

Big Idea:	If the subject is singular, the verb must be singular. If the subject is plural, the verb must be plural.

Singular	Plural
1. The boy is working hard in school.	The boys are working hard in school.
2. She is working hard in school.	They are working hard in school.
3. I am studying for a test.	We are studying for a test.
4. She was studying for a test.	They were studying for a test.

Singular	Plural
1. The boy likes pepperoni pizza.	The boys like pepperoni pizza.
2. The girl talks to her friends on her cell phone.	The girls talk to their friends on their cell phones.
3. The boy enjoys classical music.	The boys enjoy classical music.
4. The girl dreams of rafting through the Grand Canyon.	The girls dream of rafting through the Grand Canyon.
5. The boy mows lawns to buy a motorcycle.	The boys mow lawns to buy motorcycles.
6. The girl fixes computers to give them to families who need one.	The girls fix computers to give them to families who need one.

NOTE: To make a noun plural, we usually add an **s**.
        To make a verb singular, we usually add an **s**.

Big Idea:	If the subject is singular, the verb must be singular.
	If the subject is plural, the verb must be plural.

If two or more subjects are joined by **and**, use a plural verb.

1. <u>Alligators</u> and <u>porcupines</u> do not make great pets.
   (Singular: An alligator does not make a great pet.)

2. My <u>aunt</u> and my <u>uncle</u> are traveling to Turkey.
   (Singular: My aunt is traveling to Turkey.)

3. The adventurous <u>girls</u> and their <u>mother</u> were diving into the icy lake.
   (Singular: Their mother was diving into the icy lake.)

4. The house <u>keys</u> and the mailbox <u>key</u> hang by the door.
   (Singular: The mailbox key hangs by the door.)

5. The <u>performer</u> and his <u>dog</u> were jumping on the trampoline.
   (Singular: The performer was jumping on the trampoline.)

Big Idea:	If the subject is singular, the verb must be singular. If the subject is plural, the verb must be plural.

If the subjects are joined by **or** or **nor**, the verb must agree with the **nearest** subject.

1. The girl or the girl's <u>friends</u> practice soccer every day.

   The girl's friends or the <u>girl</u> practices soccer every day.

2. Either my brother or my <u>sisters</u> are going to clean the garage.

   Either my sisters or my <u>brother</u> is going to clean the garage.

3. Are my <u>teammates</u> or my coach responsible for the accident?

   Is my <u>coach</u> or my teammates responsible for the accident?

4. Neither the measuring spoons nor the <u>bowl</u> needs to be washed.

   Neither the bowl nor the measuring <u>spoons</u> need to be washed.

5. Neither the hockey players nor the <u>coach</u> is aware of the final score.

   Neither the coach nor the hockey <u>players</u> are aware of the final score.

| **Big Idea:** | If the subject is singular, the verb must be singular. If the subject is plural, the verb must be plural. |

Be sure that your subject and verb agree when they are separated by other words.

1. The <u>stores</u> on the main street of town look deserted.

2. My <u>sister</u>, in spite of many practice sessions, was not ready for the spelling bee.

3. His mystery <u>books</u>, especially his first book, were best sellers.

4. The <u>teacher</u>, together with his eager students, is flying model airplanes.

5. The <u>man</u> with all the sports cars lives on the next block.

6. The <u>people</u> who eat at that restaurant write for the newspaper.

7. <u>Natalie</u>, a singer and dancer, is taking good care of her health.

Big Idea:	If the subject is singular, the verb must be singular.
	If the subject is plural, the verb must be plural.

The words below require special attention when deciding whether to use singular or plural verbs.

Singular		Plural	Singular or Plural
anybody	neither	both	all
anyone	nobody	few	any
anything	no one	many	enough
each	one	others	more
either	somebody	several	most
everybody	someone		none
everyone	something		some

1. <u>Both</u> of the boys enjoy skateboarding and rollerblading.

2. <u>Each</u> of the bus drivers is working hard to keep the transit system on schedule.

3. <u>Several</u> have saved enough money for the field trip.

4. <u>Some</u> have seen a butterfly emerge from its cocoon.

5. <u>Somebody</u> has left his or her backpack on the bus.

6. <u>Few</u> are voting for Mike for student body president.

7. <u>None</u> of the four possibilities is the correct answer.

| **Big Idea:** | If the subject is singular, the verb must be singular.
If the subject is plural, the verb must be plural. |

Be careful when the sentence begins with **There** or **Here**.

1. There are many <u>stoplights</u>.

   There is a <u>stoplight</u>.

2. There are several <u>cars</u> in the intersection.

   There is one <u>car</u> in the intersection.

3. Here are two <u>ambulances</u>.

   Here is an <u>ambulance</u>.

4. Here are four <u>paramedics</u>.

   Here is a <u>paramedic</u>.

Big Idea:	If the subject is singular, the verb must be singular. If the subject is plural, the verb must be plural.

The words below are called collective nouns. A collective noun refers to two or more people or animals acting or being treated as one. When that is true, the collective noun is usually singular.

Collective nouns include:

audience	crowd
company	jury
government	tribe
society	college
board	family
couple	panel
group	troop
team	committee
class	flock
school	

1. The <u>company</u> builds skyscrapers.

2. The <u>audience</u> applauds at every opportunity.

3. The <u>government</u> provides many important services.

4. The <u>family</u> of monkeys chatters noisily.

5. The <u>crowd</u> waits for the parade to begin.

6. The <u>jury</u> deliberates in secret.

V